THE MEMORY BANK

By Martin Duberman

Charles Francis Adams, 1807–1886

In White America

The Antislavery Vanguard:
New Essays on the Abolitionists (editor)

James Russell Lowell

The Uncompleted Past

The Memory Bank

THE MEMORY BANK

By
Martin
Duberman

THE
DIAL
PRESS
NEW
YORK
1970

For Louise and Lew Lehrman

THE MEMORY BANK *was first presented at Tambellini's Gate Theatre, New York City, on January 11, 1970, with the following cast:*

THE RECORDER: *A History*

ANDREWS	Fred Stewart
SMYTH	Jeff David

THE ELECTRIC MAP: *A Melodrama*

TED	Laurence Luckinbill
JIM	Gil Rogers

Produced by
Davis Weinstock, Michael Pantaleoni,
Lewis E. Lehrman

Directed by
Harold Stone

Settings and Costumes by
Fred Voelpel

Lighting by
Paul Sullivan

Sound Created by
Gary Harris

INTRODUCTION

American playwrighting, right now, is going through many changes, and what lies ahead—the styles, the ideas —is very much unknown. There is a general distrust of words, too many of them having been used to say too many familiar things for too long. There is a quiet fear of the production companies, which (as part of that distrust of words) have been minimizing the role of the writer in the theatre. There is an increased sense of stage as a side effect of such production theatre. There is a disinclination toward specific content, a part of the rebellion against naturalism and traditional rationalism. There is a seeking out of theatre ways equivalent to pop art and pop music—theatre ways plugged in to today's computer sensibility.

Martin Duberman's *The Recorder* and *The Electric Map* were as into these changes as any good plays (there weren't many) when they were produced in New York in early 1970. What made them extraordinary, beyond just that, was their sheer *intelligence*. Intelligence is as rare in the theatre as it is anywhere else—so rare that when you come upon it, it's like a glass of iced water in the middle of a desert: incredibly refreshing but so long done without you've forgotten that it should be a normal part of living. The power of these two plays to drive your mind is part of their fascination.

They have many things in common but "history" describes their overriding partnership; the plays are about history in all its senses.

History as an academic discipline: *The Recorder* involves a historian researching his subject and the questionable validity of such research. *The Electric Map* is set at a "national monument" at Gettysburg and uses the Civil War as both parallel and counterpoint.

They are about personal history, that is, history as a man's past, wondering whether the past can be recalled with any accuracy at all. There is more than a trace of Pirandello in this idea but then Pirandello hasn't exclusive rights to the question, *what happened?*

The plays are also satires of academic history (about which Duberman must know more than a little, being a Professor of History at Princeton). Smyth, the historian in *The Recorder,* is writing a book which will present as fact what he is studying rather emotionally, and what he is being told with some inconsistency. *The Electric Map* mocks Civil War history, which is a popular hobby for super-America and an industry for flag-waving historians.

The plays are also about the machinery of memory (and memory, of course, is history). The title *The Memory Bank* relates the idea of history to the computer. The machines in the plays symbolize the *human* memory bank—the brain—not only as a mechanism that stores information as a computer does in *its* memory bank, but one that does so with emotional distortion; a mechanism subject to neurosis, represented by the breakdown of the memory machines in both plays.

The Recorder, a title referring to both Smyth and his tape recorder, opens with mechanical difficulties, stating both plays' theme (unstable memory-history mechanisms) at the outset. As it proceeds, neither character exactly remembers what happened or even what was just said and the tape recorder itself is no more reliable. In fact, Duberman has written the play so carefully that we grow spookily uncertain about what we've heard ourselves. So he makes the play about our memories too.

In *The Electric Map,* the brothers disagree about the facts of their shared past. Had Jim seen the map before (as Ted recalls) or not (as Jim recalls)? Did Jim run away from home (as he believes) or was he expelled (as Ted believes)? Men remember what they want to remember. The haywire map symbolizes haywire memories. It is also a spectacular visual device.

There are some flaws in this play. Ted's drinking is a trite mechanism to get him to say the unsayable, but his upset would have explained that anyhow. The analogy between the Civil War and the war between *these* brothers is coy, even more so when it is extended as it is, implicitly, to the war between individualists and conformists, dreamers and realists, artists and non-creators, homosexuals and heterosexuals. The message that all men should love each other is sentimental.

Homosexuality is still another theme that the plays share. They both suggest that social disapproval forces homosexuals to play secret, humiliating games. This is more subtle in *The Recorder,* which is a more subtle play in general. Smyth and Andrews are going through a courtship of sorts. The game they play is a romantic one. Andrews is passive, coy, and secretive. He has-is what Smyth wants (information about the subject of the research, who may very well be Andrews himself). Smyth is the chaser, subservient because of his desire—as all suitors are—using every possible guile to seduce Andrews into revealing everything, the equivalent of sexual compliance. At the same time, of course, *any* interview is a kind of seduction scene. The thread of homosexuality in *The Recorder* surfaces only once, when the men make a dinner date, but even then the appointment could be perfectly nonsexual, the second step of a power game between two people. The breathlessness and uncertainty of it contribute secretly and cannily to the play's mysteries.

So you aren't sure of it. The suggestion is modulated, but one of many careful ambiguities in both plays. This scheme is exemplary of Duberman's care, craftsmanship, imagination, controlled surrealism, clean language, and sheer intelligence. These plays are as lean and modern as anything written in their period.

New York City   Martin Gottfried
April, 1970

THE RECORDER:

A History

A play for TWO MEN *and a* TAPE RECORDER.
The RECORDER *is on the table.* SMYTH
is fiddling with it as the curtain rises.

SMYTH

Huh! You'd think after a couple of hundred times
I'd be able to thread the damn thing.

ANDREWS

Take your time.

SMYTH

To tell you the truth, I'd just about given up hope that
you'd see me. I'm grateful to you for letting me come by.

ANDREWS

I admire persistence.

SMYTH

I didn't mean to plague you.

ANDREWS

It was my secretaries you plagued. But eventually
word does filter through to me.

SMYTH

When you didn't answer my third letter, I got
a bit rattled.

5

ANDREWS

I was making enquiries.

SMYTH

I understand. You must get all kinds of requests.

ANDREWS

All kinds.

SMYTH

(Still fiddling with the MACHINE*)*
Damn! I seem to be all thumbs today.

ANDREWS

You have quite a reputation for one so young.

SMYTH

Thank you.

ANDREWS

This book, of course, will boost it still further.

SMYTH

I hadn't thought of it that way.

ANDREWS

Oh my. Pure as well as accomplished.

SMYTH

I think the book will be timely.

ANDREWS

You've talked to many others, have you?

SMYTH

Oh literally hundreds, sir. You're the last.

ANDREWS

(Pointing to the TAPE RECORDER*)*
And did you cart *that* with you everywhere?

SMYTH

Yes. It's not very heavy . . . Ah! There. That does it.

(He looks up at ANDREWS*)*

I hope this isn't going to bother you too much.

ANDREWS

Can't really tell. I've never used one before.
I do feel self-conscious.

SMYTH

You'll forget it's there after a few minutes. That's the
theory anyway. Frankly, I've never gotten used to it.

ANDREWS

Then why do you use it?

SMYTH

I want to get what you say straight. I've got a rotten
memory. Funny in a historian, isn't it? Can't keep a fact
in my head. It's safer using the machine. That way
I'll be sure it's accurate.

ANDREWS

But it might not come out right. I am a little nervous.

SMYTH

About the machine.

ANDREWS

No, about it coming out right. I've forgotten a lot.
I hope that the

(Pause)

talking

(Pause)

will bring back—

7

SMYTH

Don't worry. You'll relax once we get started.

(*Strained pause*)

ANDREWS

Shall I talk now?

SMYTH

I haven't turned it on. All set?

ANDREWS

I suppose.

SMYTH

Let's start right in then.

ANDREWS

Fine.

SMYTH

I'll stop it after a minute just to be sure we're recording.

(HE *turns on the* RECORDER *and returns to his seat.*)

Any time you're ready.

ANDREWS

Should I just talk?

SMYTH

Whatever makes you most comfortable.

ANDREWS

Is it recording?

SMYTH

Should be. Would it help if I asked direct questions?

8

ANDREWS
What do you particularly want to know?

SMYTH
Well, I guess most crucial would be— it's so hard to
know what's finally going to be important . . . Why not
just start talking about him. Anything you happen
to remember.

ANDREWS
I remember next to nothing about his early life.

SMYTH
Anything. It might be important.

ANDREWS
You mean like his schooling?

SMYTH
If that's as far back as you can go.

ANDREWS
(After a pause)
I can see him on a beach. He was three or four.
Beautiful baby. Snow-white hair.

SMYTH
With his family?

ANDREWS
I suppose so. There's something about his sister.
Probably not true. I shouldn't say it.

SMYTH
Please. You have my promise. This is strictly for my own
information. Not a word will go into print, without
your permission.

9

ANDREWS

I believe you. Still, one can't be sure. I do feel
a responsibility.

SMYTH

I know what you mean. It's important to get
everything as accurate as possible. That's why I use the
machine. I don't want to have to rely on memory.

ANDREWS

Well. There was some story about his sister at the
beach. They loved each other very much, you know.
Everyone in the family said so; always. She was left to
take care of him for a while. I don't think she was
more than eight. He was very fair-skinned. She kept
pouring water over his little body. To keep him cool,
you know. She'd go back and forth to the ocean, filling
her pail. Kept pouring it over him. He got a very
nasty burn. Second-degree, I think they said. She was
only trying to keep him cool. Poor child.

SMYTH

Who?

ANDREWS

Who?

SMYTH

You said "poor child." I wasn't sure who you meant.

ANDREWS

Oh. Him. I suppose. I did say "poor child"?

SMYTH

Yes. I'm quite sure.

10

ANDREWS

Curious.

(Brightening)

Well, if I did, it'll be on the machine.

SMYTH

Oh, Christ! I forgot to check if we're recording!

(Jumps up and goes to the MACHINE.
HE *clicks it off)*

I'll just go back a bit. To be sure we're recording. This machine is bad on reproducing voices. You won't sound a bit like yourself.

ANDREWS

I've never heard myself.

SMYTH

Then you won't know how differently you sound.

ANDREWS

You'll be able to tell, though.

*(*SMYTH *starts to rewind the* MACHINE*)*

SMYTH

When I bought this machine I looked for a microphone with a sensitive pickup. So that people wouldn't have to hold it right in front of them. This one's very good. You can put it in the corner of a room and speak in your normal voice and it picks it right up. But the quality of the sound isn't so hot. Since I'm not recording music, though, I don't care. As long as the typist can hear the words.

ANDREWS

It must have been expensive.

11

SMYTH
(Stopping the RECORDER*)*
That's more than enough. Remember—it won't sound
like you. I mean the quality. Your voice has a lot
more resonance.

*(*HE *turns on the* MACHINE*)*

MACHINE
"She'd go back and forth to the ocean, filling her pail.
Kept pouring it over him. He got a very nasty
burn. Second-degree, I think they said. She was only
trying to keep him cool. Poor child."

*(*SMYTH *clicks off the* MACHINE*)*

SMYTH
There's the "poor child."

ANDREWS
Yes. You were right. It didn't sound like me.

SMYTH
But you'd never heard yourself.

ANDREWS
You know: what I thought I'd sound like.
(Pause)
It's working then?

SMYTH
Yes. We'll be able to relax now. I won't stop it again.
*(*HE *clicks the* MACHINE *back on and returns
to his seat)*
Now let's see . . . where were we?

12

ANDREWS

I'm not happy about that.

SMYTH

But that's not the way you really sound.

ANDREWS

Not my voice. The story about the beach. I'm not at all sure it's true.

SMYTH

Can you recall when you first heard it?

ANDREWS

Heard it? I was there.

SMYTH

On the beach?!

ANDREWS

No, of course not. But it was retold in his family a thousand times. You must have heard it yourself.

SMYTH

I have, in fact. But your version is different. My accounts involved his mother, not the sister.

ANDREWS

That's absurd. A grown woman would never have done such a thing.

SMYTH

It does seem improbable. How did the mother strike you?

ANDREWS

Certainly not cruel. Far from cruel. She adored the boy. She was very beautiful.

13

SMYTH

What's your first memory of her?

(ANDREWS *thinks; then becomes embarrassed, agitated*)

ANDREWS

This kind of raking up. I really have my doubts, you know. What's the point?

SMYTH

I'm trying to understand what made him tick. I want to find out everything I can.

(Pause)

ANDREWS

I only remember a few things. Without all the rest, they can't be trusted. They'll loom too large.

SMYTH

Each person remembers a little. I put it all together.

(The MACHINE *squeaks)*

Hmm. I can't figure that out. It happens at the damnedest times. No pattern to it.

ANDREWS

Maybe it needs oil.

SMYTH

Oh, no! The manual says never to oil it. It has a sealed lubrication system.

(The MACHINE *squeaks again)*

ANDREWS

Then maybe it isn't level. The least thing throws them off. Maybe you'd better take notes instead.

*(SMYTH *gets up*)*

14

SMYTH

Let's try moving it.

> (HE *clicks the* MACHINE *off and starts to move it*)

ANDREWS

Watch the cord! It's going to pull the microphone out.

SMYTH

Oh, yes. Thank you.

> (HE *readjusts the cord, then turns the* MACHINE *back on.* HE *listens a few seconds*)

Seems okay. You were right about leveling. Seems to have done it.

> (HE *goes back to his seat*)

You were going to tell me your first recollections of the mother.

ANDREWS

I think I was not going to tell you.

SMYTH

I give you my word this is all strictly confidential.

ANDREWS

> (*Looking at the* MACHINE)

Notes are better. That's all they are, and everyone knows it: traces. They can be denied, destroyed.

SMYTH

The tape is yours. I'll have it typed up, and then I'll send you both the tape and the typescript.

ANDREWS

How will I know there isn't a carbon?

15

SMYTH
(Embarrassed)
I guess you'll have to take my word.

ANDREWS
I don't even know you. Not really, that is.

SMYTH
It does come down to trust.
(Pause)

ANDREWS
You *will* ask my permission if you want to quote
something from your carbon?

SMYTH
You have my word.

ANDREWS
Mm-hmm.
(Pause)
Well. The boy was a good deal older. Thirteen or
fourteen. He got the idea one day to write a story.

SMYTH
Excuse me, I had hoped you would tell me about his
mother.

ANDREWS
(Sternly)
I'm about to.

SMYTH
Oh, I'm sorry.

ANDREWS
It was a moralistic little tale. About a girl named Jane
who tried to be good but couldn't. He was very excited

16

when he finished writing it and ran in to show it to his
mother. She read it and then turned to him angrily:
"You should be outside playing with the rest of the boys
in the street," she said. "If you were a real boy, that's
where you'd be." The boy looked as if he would faint.

SMYTH

Could you backtrack just a bit. There's something I
didn't get.

ANDREWS

You don't have to. The machine will.

SMYTH

Just to get it straight myself, for the conversation.

ANDREWS

So you can ask the right questions.

SMYTH

Exactly.

ANDREWS

He had written a little story about Jane, you see.

SMYTH

No, I understand that part. I meant the mother's anger.
Why was she angry? What was she angry at?

ANDREWS

I really don't know. Maybe *she* didn't.

SMYTH

But what would you guess?

ANDREWS

I couldn't begin to.

17

SMYTH
(Pressing him)

Was she worried that he might not be—well—what do you call it—a "regular fellow"?

ANDREWS

Maybe.

SMYTH

You think that did worry her.

ANDREWS

Maybe. Otherwise why would she have said it?

SMYTH

Said what?

ANDREWS

About playing in the street more.

SMYTH

She wanted him to play in the street more. With the rest of the boys.

ANDREWS

No, it seems to me that's exactly what worried her. He was out in the street so much with *that* kind of boy.

SMYTH

What kind?

ANDREWS

The ones he would play with.

SMYTH

I'm afraid you've lost me.

ANDREWS

Oh, well.

(Pause)

18

SMYTH

You think then—just to clear this up—that his mother disapproved of the crowd of boys he was hanging out with. On the streets.

ANDREWS

I really couldn't say. It was so long ago.

SMYTH

I know how hard it is to recall these things. It must be forty years ago, isn't it? At least.

ANDREWS

I should think. Something like that. You probably know better than I.

SMYTH

Sometimes I think I know him very well. Then it turns out there are whole episodes I've never even heard of. This story about Jane, for example.

ANDREWS

Remember, I didn't want to tell it. I have no confidence in it.

SMYTH

Why don't we try it again. If you don't mind. Tell it to me again.

ANDREWS
(Sighs)

It's like this. He was not the sort of boy—mind you, this is only as I remember him—who was much for the usual horseplay and sports. Now and then he'd enjoy it. In fact he was a good athlete. Quite good, now that I think about it. He used to win cups in summer camp. Best all-around midget. That sort of thing. But he liked other

19

things, too. Words, any kind of words. In books, in talk.
He liked putting words together.

SMYTH

So he started to write stories.

ANDREWS

Yes. There we are. He wrote that story about Jane. He
must have been a tot still. Couldn't have been more than
seven.

SMYTH

This is the same story about Jane you just described?
The moralistic one?

ANDREWS
(Surprised)
Were there two Jane stories? Huh! I'd always assumed
there'd only been the one.

SMYTH

I didn't know of *any*. That is before today.

ANDREWS

Then why do you refer to two?

SMYTH

The first one you said he wrote when he was about
thirteen or fourteen. And now this last one you
mentioned you said he wrote when he was about seven.

ANDREWS

I only know of one Jane story.

SMYTH

But you did say earlier he had been thirteen or fourteen.

ANDREWS

Not as I remember. I don't see how I could have.

20

SMYTH

I could've sworn you said thirteen or four—Well, no matter. The machine will have it in any case.

ANDREWS

Perhaps we should rewind and see.

SMYTH

It would be difficult to find the exact spot. I can sort it all out later. It's all there. Anyway, you are now sure he was about seven when he wrote that story.

ANDREWS

Yes, quite sure. I can't swear to it, of course. You know what funny tricks memory can play. But I am reasonably sure he was seven.

SMYTH

Fine. Let's get back then to his mother's reaction. Apparently she didn't like his playing in the streets so much.

ANDREWS

In truth, I think it depended on the boys he was with. Actually, he had several sets of friends. Some the mother liked and some she didn't.

SMYTH

Which did she like?

ANDREWS
(Thinking)

I wish I could be sure. It seems to me the one she really *didn't* like was the girl across the street.

SMYTH

Not Jane?

21

ANDREWS

No, no. You've got that wrong. The *story* was about a
girl named Jane.

SMYTH

That's what I'd thought.

ANDREWS

Yes, that's right. The *story* was about a girl named Jane.

SMYTH

And the girl across the street?

ANDREWS

Quite something else. She had her hooks into him, you
know. Girls aren't very old when they start thinking of
marriage.

SMYTH

Yes, but seven—!

ANDREWS

The suburbs. You know how it is. In any case, I
wouldn't say seven. No, I couldn't be sure of seven. Not
the girl across the street.

SMYTH

She was older then?

ANDREWS

Yes, that was part of the trouble. She was much too old
for him. Kept him inside all the time. That's what the
mother objected to, you see.

SMYTH

She wanted him out in the street with the boys.

22

ANDREWS

Right. Playing games. That sort of thing.

SMYTH

Would he and the girl write together?

ANDREWS

They mostly played bridge. Even at lunchtime, during
school break. Bridge, bridge, bridge. Became very good
at it. A lifelong hobby of his.

SMYTH

Yes. I'd heard that.

ANDREWS

He put himself through college playing bridge.

SMYTH

Really? But he didn't need to do that. He was a wealthy
boy.

ANDREWS

He *wanted* to do it.
(Pause)
Bridge is an intricate game.
(Pause)
Do you play?

SMYTH

No, not very well.
(Pause)
You and he were roommates in college, weren't you?

ANDREWS

Yes. That is, after the freshman year. *That* may be the
most interesting story of all. No memory problem there.

23

SMYTH

Good.

ANDREWS

But it is painful for me to recall.

SMYTH

I understand.

(ANDREWS *is silent*)

SMYTH

(Trying to coax)

Painful episodes are often important.

ANDREWS

For your book, you mean.

SMYTH

Yes, exactly.

(Pause)

But you know I once dropped this whole project. Gave it up entirely for three months. It was after I talked to a woman in Delaware. The more she talked about the "good old days," the more she drank. By the time it was over I couldn't make any sense of what she way saying. I felt terrible, encouraging her to look back. It was like picking scabs off old wounds.

ANDREWS

Inhuman. Why do you do it?

SMYTH

We have to find out the truth.

ANDREWS

For posterity, I suppose.

24

SMYTH

We must hold on to past experiences. It's all we have to guide us. Without it we'd be like amnesia victims, no moorings at all.

ANDREWS

Each day would be brand-new.

SMYTH

Exactly. Think how disconcerting that would be. Having to start fresh each day.

> *(Noises from the* MACHINE*; the reel has come to an end)*

The reel has ended.

> *(*SMYTH *goes to the* MACHINE *and starts to turn over the reel)*

ANDREWS

It must have missed that last part. About amnesia.

SMYTH

That doesn't matter. It was just me, gabbing.

> *(Laughs)*

I'm not interested in recording me.

ANDREWS

Those reels aren't very long.

SMYTH

They come in various lengths. I put on a short one. I wasn't sure how long we'd be.

> *(*HE *laughs; trying to charm* ANDREWS *into further reminiscence)*

But you're a mine of information.

25

ANDREWS

No one was closer to him, after all.

SMYTH
(*Finishing up with the* MACHINE)
That does it. I've turned it over to the other side.
(HE *goes back to his seat*)
Now. Just pick up where you were.

ANDREWS

We were talking about bridge, weren't we?

SMYTH

No, we'd finished with that.

ANDREWS

Oh, had we?

SMYTH

I know—we were talking about college. Something you said was very vivid.

ANDREWS

I doubt if it's the sort of thing you want. After all, he's a public figure. This is pretty private stuff. As I say, we were close.

SMYTH

I promise you it will stay private. I want to know everything I can, but I certainly don't intend printing everything.

ANDREWS

Then why know it?

SMYTH

I want to understand why he acted the way he did.

26

ANDREWS

Just describe his actions, his public career. That's what's important. That's what's affected history.

SMYTH

But it all might have happened differently. I mean, if he'd been a different kind of man, he might have made different decisions, affected history differently.

ANDREWS

Historians shouldn't deal in "ifs," it seems to me. If he'd been different he wouldn't have affected history at all. If he'd been able to screw that girl, he'd never have been a public figure.

SMYTH

The girl across the street?

ANDREWS

No, the girl in college. Joan I think her name was. Maybe I'm thinking of Jane again. Joan? Yes, Joan. She came up for the big freshman weekend. Very sexed-up girl. Everybody knew it. They'd been dating off and on. This was supposed to be the big culmination. She'd promised him that if he invited her up for the weekend, she'd have sex with him. He'd told everybody. It was like the wedding night. Everybody knew they were going to do it. There was practically a crowd waiting for them when they came out of the room.

SMYTH

What room?

ANDREWS

Don't know. Funny, everything else is so vivid. Some freshman's room. We had a big party there after the

27

dance. About a dozen couples. Lots of drinking.
Something called "purple passion"—gin and grape juice.
There was a huge vat of it. An aluminum vat. With
large cakes of ice floating in it. We slopped the stuff
down. One girl got sick, I remember. Vomited down the
stairwell. Quite a sight. Splashed down the stairs.

SMYTH

It wasn't Joan.

ANDREWS

No, no. They were curled up on the floor. Making out.
Everybody was. But we had our eyes on them. We were
all virgins—except Joan. It was a different generation;
you know. He was going to be the first. That night. We
could hardly wait. Finally they got up and went into the
back room. I think three of us had orgasms on the spot.

SMYTH

Doesn't sound like the kids nowadays.

ANDREWS

Sex was a big deal for us. It took a lot of planning and
work. Sometimes we had to throw in an engagement
ring. The kids today would think we're crazy. For them
it's like taking a leak.

SMYTH

They wouldn't believe your freshman prom.

ANDREWS

They'd believe it. They just wouldn't care. All those
fools in the past. Bury it, forget it. You don't expect
them to read your book, do you?

28

SMYTH

I don't know. I never thought about it. I guess not.

ANDREWS

Why would they? What's it got to tell them?

SMYTH

It could show them how differently people behave.

ANDREWS

So?

SMYTH

It would open up a range of possibilities.

(ANDREWS *laughs*)

ANDREWS

We all know there are insane asylums. But we don't keep visiting them. Who's going to read your book?

SMYTH

Non-fiction sells well. Better than fiction.

ANDREWS *(Thoughtfully)*

I wonder where Joan would fit.

SMYTH

You didn't make her up?!

ANDREWS

I told you how vivid she was. I can see her coming out of that room. Strange expression on her face. Hard to read. Something like his mother's when she saw that story about Jane. His face was less complicated. He was upset. Very upset.

SMYTH

Did he say why?

ANDREWS

Not then. Nobody questioned them. But he said
something later to a few of us that they had decided to
wait; that Joan was having a period; something like that.

(HE *looks at the* MACHINE)

Hasn't the tape ended?

SMYTH

(*Getting half out of the chair to look at the*
MACHINE)

No, we still have a ways to go.

ANDREWS

This side seems longer than the other.

SMYTH

It does, doesn't it.

ANDREWS

We must be on pot.

SMYTH

I beg your pardon?

ANDREWS

Pot distorts the sense of time. Haven't you ever smoked?

SMYTH

No. Have you?

ANDREWS

No. Well, what else do you want for the time capsule?

SMYTH

Did he say anything to you later about Joan?

ANDREWS

He said they'd made out on the floor. That he'd come in
his handkerchief. She'd understood. She had veen very
understanding.

(Pause)

SMYTH
(Embarrassed; confused)
What is it she had been understanding about?

ANDREWS

About his being afraid. She said it didn't matter that he
couldn't get an erection. That often happened the first
time. No—wait a minute. I think I've got that confused.
That wasn't part of the episode with Joan. It seems to
me it was earlier. No; perhaps later. With that call girl, I
think it was, in Florida. The taxi driver had taken them
to this little house on the outskirts of Palm Beach. Yes, it
was a house, not a call girl. All the girls—there must
have been five or six—were sitting around a small room
rocking slowly in their chairs. Nobody said anything.
We sat down. The girls just kept rocking. Finally one of
them broke into a laugh. "Come on, boys," she said,
"make a choice. We can't spend the whole day." I
grabbed the girl nearest me and we went into a back
room. She dropped her robe as soon as we got into the
room. Then she asked me what I wanted. Everything
had a different price. "Round the world" was the big
one; I think it cost twenty dollars. I told her I only had
seven dollars on me. She didn't believe me, so I let her
look in my wallet. She said for seven dollars she could
only screw me. We tried for what seemed like hours.

31

And we weren't on pot. Finally she said she'd blow me a little to help me work it up, but that I wasn't to tell the madame or any of my friends or she'd catch hell—for seven bucks she was supposed to give me a straight screw and that was it. The blow job didn't help. She was nice about it. Said not to worry, that married men often came in and couldn't do it either. She squirted some kind of ointment around the opening of my cock. Then she wrapped it in gauze, and put a rubber band around it. She said when my friends saw it they'd think I had screwed her.

> *(Long pause;* SMYTH *is nonplussed;* ANDREWS *sits very calmly)*

I really can't see why you want to know all this.

SMYTH
> *(Confused; hesitant)*

Well . . . it's fascinating. It . . . uh . . . helps to explain a great deal.

ANDREWS

It does? Like what?

SMYTH

I think it tells me a lot about your—about the—relations with women. I mean, tying that in with writing the story about Jane. And his inability to have intercourse with Joan.

ANDREWS

He had intercourse with Joan. On the floor. I told you that.

SMYTH

Didn't he say they had decided to wait? That Joan was having a period?

ANDREWS

That's what the handkerchief was for.

(Noises from the MACHINE; *the tape has ended)*

SMYTH

Damn! What a time for the tape to end.

ANDREWS

About time. We've been here forever.

(Pause)

Would you do me a favor and backtrack a bit? I'd like to hear that section on the freshman party.

(SMYTH starts to rewind the MACHINE*)*

SMYTH

Of course. I'd be glad to.

ANDREWS

I want to be sure I got it straight.

(Pause)

She was a very moralistic girl, that Jane. Mary Jane.

(SMYTH stops the MACHINE, *then starts it forward again)*

MACHINE

"She kept pouring water over his little body . . ."

SMYTH

(Startled; HE *stops* THE MACHINE*)*

I thought that section was on the other side. That was all much earlier.

33

*(ANDREWS sits quietly. SMYTH again rewinds
the MACHINE for a few seconds, then starts it
forward)*

MACHINE

". . . something to a few of us that they had decided to
wait; that Joan was having a period . . ."

*(Slight pause; then a FEMALE VOICE on the
tape)*

FEMALE VOICE

"We can't spend the whole day."

*(ANDREWS looks up startled; SMYTH stops
the MACHINE)*

ANDREWS

Who was that?

SMYTH
(Laughs)

Sorry. That sometimes happens. I re-use the tapes after
the typist makes a transcript. Sometimes they don't erase
fully. But you *had* said they decided to wait. You see it is
as I remembered it: they did not have intercourse. I
thought that was what you'd said.

ANDREWS

They did have intercourse, as I've already told you. But
not to climax. The handerchief. I was quite distinct
about that.

SMYTH
(Nervously)

Tapes don't lie.

34

ANDREWS

Neither do I.

SMYTH
(Placating)

Why don't we just try it from scratch? I can put on a new reel of tape. Or we can record right over the first version.

ANDREWS

Frankly, this is getting a little tedious. It was, after all, a minor incident. I probably should never have mentioned it. You'll be making too much of it—that he was impotent, or afraid of women, or God knows what.

SMYTH

No, nothing like that.

ANDREWS

Then what will you say?

SMYTH

Well, to the extent that I understand it—

ANDREWS

Don't be modest. It's unbecoming in an historian. Makes people doubt your word.

SMYTH

Well, it seems to me—

ANDREWS

Bad start.
(Peremptory)

Who was Jane?

SMYTH

Jane was a fictional character about whom he once wrote. When he was a child.

35

ANDREWS

Good. Turn on the tape recorder.

(SMYTH *hesitantly complies*)

Now come sit down.

(SMYTH *returns to his chair*)

Who was the real-life character?

SMYTH

Joan?

ANDREWS

You're sure you don't want to say his mother?

SMYTH

(Hesitantly)

Quite sure.

ANDREWS

You don't sound sure.

SMYTH

(More firmly)

I'm quite sure. Joan was very real to him. You made her sound very real.

ANDREWS

What made her so real?

SMYTH

Her kindness.

ANDREWS

Is the machine recording?

SMYTH

Yes.

36

ANDREWS

You're quite sure.

SMYTH

Yes.

ANDREWS

In what way was she kind?

SMYTH

She read to him. Moralistic little tales. Useful, though, when a child is growing up. And they would play games. Card games, like bridge. They were very close throughout childhood. Very close.

ANDREWS

You have the feel of it. That girl was important to him. How about as they got older?

SMYTH

He went off to college, as boys do.

(ANDREWS *laughs*)

ANDREWS

That's a nice phrase: "As boys do." I'd keep that in the book if I were you. Don't worry: the machine's got it.

SMYTH

When it came time for the freshman dance, he didn't know whether to invite her up for it or not.

ANDREWS

I don't remember saying that.

SMYTH

Those weren't your exact words. It was the impression I got. Call it intuition.

37

ANDREWS
(Brooding about it)

Yes, yes, I'd say you were right. You've got the essence of
it. Truth of mood I suppose you'd call it. Rather than
truth of fact. That's very important in good historical
writing. You have to be able to recreate the spirit of the
times. That's much more important than getting every
little fact right. Any fool can check names and dates.

SMYTH

It's the difference between pedantry and poetry.

ANDREWS

Well said.

SMYTH
(Very pleased)

But the weekend was a disaster.

(A little alarmed at his audacity)

That is, looking at it overall.

ANDREWS

Hmm. Very perceptive.

SMYTH
(Elated)

They had hoped it would prove to be the consummation
of the relationship. But they went to a wild party with
friends after the dance. Had too much gin. Besides, there
was too much fuss about the whole thing. Almost all
their friends knew they were planning to have
intercourse.

ANDREWS

Right. That, I think, *is* the key.

SMYTH

It was like performing on a stage. Enough to inhibit
anyone. When the time came he was impotent. She was
kind about it. Very kind, really. She fondled him; told
him not to worry. That made it worse.

(ANDREWS *looks up with sharp interest*)

ANDREWS

Oh?

SMYTH

It reminded him of the one time he had gone to a whore
house. He had been impotent there, too. And the
prostitute had been very understanding. She had even
put a kind of bandage on his penis, so that his friends
would think he had screwed himself bloody.

ANDREWS
(Delighted)

Excellent!

SMYTH

The memory was very painful. When Joan fondled his
penis, it brought the whole episode back. He was groggy
anyway, from the gin. So he couldn't perform. He told
her he'd been having too much sex recently—yes, he
frankly confessed that he had been screwing himself
bloody.

ANDREWS

Splendid!

SMYTH

She felt sorry for him. And angry. They never saw each
other again. He did that to people. He went on to fame
and fortune. They disappeared from history.

39

ANDREWS

You've really extracted the essence.

> *(Pause)*

Play back the very last few lines, would you? You put that so well, I'd like to try to remember it.

> *(SMYTH goes to the MACHINE, starts to rewind)*

Besides, I haven't heard how *your* voice sounds.

SMYTH

> *(Stopping the MACHINE)*

That should do it.

> *(SMYTH presses the "Forward" button)*

MACHINE

". . . again. He did that to people. He went on to fame and fortune. They disappeared from history."

> *(Another VOICE comes on the MACHINE)*

MACHINE

"You've really extracted the essence."

ANDREWS

Good Lord, it doesn't sound a bit li   're right: the reproduction is very poor.

> *(SMYTH stops the MA*

SMYTH

That last bit was *you*.

ANDREWS

Which bit?

SMYTH

"You've really extracted the essenc.

40

ANDREWS

I shouldn't be surprised. Good thing we had the machine here to get it all done.

(HE *rises*)

Well then. I think you have all you need.

SMYTH

(Hesitant)

I'd hoped you might tell me a little more about what he was like to live with.

ANDREWS

No, that's a complicated story. Not easy to grasp.

SMYTH

Perhaps another time.

ANDREWS

Perhaps. When we're fresh. It *is* an important story. Very important

SMYTH

Then may I call you again?

We might have dinner. In two weeks, say.

That would be marvelous.

ANDREWS

Yes, two weeks from tonight should be fine. Come by at seven

SMYTH

I certainly appreciate it.

ANDREWS

My pleasure.

> *(Pause, while* SMYTH *gathers up the cord, microphone, etc.)*

Interesting business, this looking back. Surprising how much it can stir up after all these years.

SMYTH

> *(Sententiously)*

Well, the only way to free ourselves from the past is to learn it.

ANDREWS

We've got you people to thank for that.

> (HE *looks at the* TAPE RECORDER; *chuckles)*

That is, you and the tape recorder. You're going to set all of us free.

> *(Pause)*

In two weeks, then.

SMYTH

Two weeks.

BLACKOUT

THE ELECTRIC MAP:

A Melodrama

Backstage at the "electric map" of the battle
of Gettysburg. The map covers the entire
upstage area, from floor to ceiling. TED *is*
above stage, fiddling with a loudspeaker.
JIM *enters stage right.* HE *is carrying a*
newspaper. HE *looks around for* TED, *finally*
spots him on the grid above stage.

            JIM
            (Calling up)

Ted!

           *(*TED *looks up, startled)*

            TED

Hey, Jim!

            JIM

What the hell are you doing up there?

            TED

Checking the wiring. Something's gone wrong with the
volume. It keeps jumping up and down. I can't figure it
out.

            JIM

Will you come down here! There's something I got to
talk to you about—and now.

45

TED

Since you're here, Jim, maybe you wouldn't mind—

JIM
(Interrupting)
Are you kiddin' me?! I got a few other things on my mind. You need an electrician, go pay for one.

(TED *starts down the ladder*)

TED

We put in a call for one three hours ago. He hasn't shown up. First the volume jumps way up. Then it goes low. Can't figure it out.

(TED *trips on a step of the ladder*)

JIM
(Sarcastic)
Don't break your neck.

TED

Funny, it's been perfect till today. I guess it's just one of those days.

JIM
(Bitterly)
Sure as hell is. One in a million.

(TED *is now on the ground*)

TED

The girl in your office didn't know where to find you.

JIM
(Agitated)
I haven't been in the office all day.

TED

Well I'm glad she got the message through to you. I was afraid she wouldn't be able to reach you.

JIM

What message?

TED

(Startled)

To come over here.

JIM

(Slowly, as if to be sure HE *understands)*

You left a message with my office for me to come over here. I see. You sent for me.

TED

Well, of course. I mean you're here, aren't you?

JIM

(Quietly)

Oh, I'm here all right.

*(*HE *puts the newspaper on the table)*

Couldn't keep me away.

TED

(Brightening at what HE *thinks is concern for him)*

Gee thanks, Jim. It's important or I wouldn't have asked you to come.

JIM

You know, for once I agree with you. It *is* important.

TED

(Confused)

But you haven't heard what it is yet.

47

JIM
(Glancing at the newspaper)

I can read.

TED
(Alarmed)

Read? What do you mean? Read what?

    *(HE moves toward the newspaper. JIM
    stands, blocking access)*

JIM

Your face, your face. I can read it in your face.

TED
(Relieved)

Oh!

    (HE laughs nervously)

Yeah, I guess that's the way it is with brothers.

    (HE fingers his face)

So it shows in my face, huh?

JIM

You look tense.

TED
(Trying to slough it off)

Not really. Just a little problem.

    (Changing the subject)

How's Ann?

JIM

Fine.

TED

Good. Glad to hear it. And the kids?

48

JIM
(Impatient)

Fine. We're all fine.

TED

Good. Glad to hear it. Haven't seen them in a long time.
(Pause. JIM *folds his arms over his chest)*

JIM

So.

(Pause)

TED

I miss seeing those kids.

JIM

Look, are you gonna tell me why you asked me here?
(Trace of menace)

Or should I tell you why I came.

TED
(Nervous laugh)

Isn't that one and the same thing?

JIM

It might be.

TED
(Looking around; evasive)

I'll bet you don't recognize the old place.

JIM

Of course I don't recognize it. I've never been here
before.

49

TED

What? Sure you have! Mama used to take us here when we were kids.

JIM

Nope, not me. Never been inside the place.

TED

I could of sworn you came along with mama and me.
(Pause)
Well—what do you think of it?

JIM

Reminds me of a morgue.

TED

Oh wait till you see it when the show starts! It becomes a whole different world. You won't believe it!

JIM

Never have.

TED

Huh?

JIM

Nothing.
(Pause)
How's Warren?

TED

Warren's fine. Just fine.

JIM

So we're all fine. Terrific.

TED

Stay and see the show! It's about to start.

JIM

I don't have much time.

TED
(Cajoling)

Boy! If you were in New York I'll bet you wouldn't go
see the Statue of Liberty.

JIM

I might. If it was in the neighborhood.
(Laughs)

I wouldn't give up a piece of ass for it, if that's what you
mean.

TED

It's not what I mean.

JIM

Didn't think so.
(Pause)

TED

Come on. I'll give you the grand tour.
(TED *moves up the metal stairway toward
the control booth)*

JIM

The hell you will. We've got some talking to do.

TED

This is the control booth. This is where I run the show
from.
(Gesturing behind the map)

C'mon, I'll show you the auditorium.
(JIM *hesitates)*

C'mon, c'mon.

51

(JIM reluctantly follows TED upstage right. TED pulls back a corner of the curtain so JIM can see into the "auditorium" of the Map. JIM jumps back)

JIM
(Angrily)

There are people out there!

TED
(Smug)

Why sure there are people out there. That's the auditorium. How many people do you think that auditorium holds?

JIM

No idea.

TED

Well take a guess.

JIM

Three hundred.

TED
(Pleased)

You're way off. Guess again.

JIM

Who knows. Three-fifty.

TED

On the button!
(Slyly)

That is, seven years ago.

JIM

Huh?

TED

Did you see those two strips of chairs down the side
aisles?

> (JIM *starts poking around the "Private
> Area"* TED *has made for himself beneath the
> stairway of the Map.* HE *opens* TED*'s
> footlocker, picks up the magazines lying
> on a table next to* TED*'s armchair, etc.*)

That was wasted space when I came on the job seven
years ago. It was my idea to put those two rows in. And
now
> *(Dramatically)*
we seat *four-hundred and seventeen* people!

JIM
> *(Bored)*
Is that a fact.

TED

That's right—four-hundred and seventeen people. And
filled every performance.

JIM

Don't look filled.

TED

I mean during the tourist season. Summers there's not a
seat in the house. Not one.

JIM

Sounds like somebody's making a good buck. Not you, I
suppose.

53

TED

I do important work here. This is a national monument.

JIM

Mmm. Those jobs pay low. Maybe you ought to look around for some other kind of work. Maybe even leave this town. The change might do you good.

TED

I would never leave the Map. During the summer we do eight shows a day here. That's three thousand, three hundred, thirty-six people see this show every day.

JIM

The same show, eight times a day?

TED

(Indignant)

You don't think we'd change it, do you?!

JIM

(Quietly amused)

I guess not.

TED

You may not believe this, Jimmy, but when I came here they were doing this show live! Can you imagine?!

JIM

Yeah, if I try.

TED

No, no, you don't understand. The guy who had this job before me would do the show *live*.

JIM

You told me that.

54

TED

He'd just talk into the mike, throwing in this or that, making all kinds of mistakes.

> (JIM *unscrews one of the bulbs from its socket on the Map, and examines it*)

I said, "Oh no! I take this job, it's going to be done *right*. The Battle of Gettysburg happened one way and only one way and that's the way we tell it!"

JIM
> *(Ironic)*

Good boy!

TED
> *(Missing the irony)*

Pretty gutsy, huh?

JIM

You told 'em, all right.

TED

So how do you think we did it?

JIM

Did what?

TED

Got the battle letter-perfect?

JIM

Beats me. Hired a new general?

> (THEY *laugh, then exchange boyish punches*)

TED
> *(Still giggling)*

No.

55

(Switching to a serious tone)

I automated the whole show! Every line, every light cue is electronically coordinated!

JIM

No kidding.

TED

Every show is just like every other one.

JIM

That's terrific. Of course, people only see the show once.

TED

(Feigned shock; then patronizing)

Jim: you don't seem to understand that this is a national monument.

JIM

Yeah, so you said.

TED

People come here from all over the country. And I mean *all* over. Just last week—now you might not believe this—we had a couple here from Hawaii!

JIM

(Unenthused)

Is that right?

TED

Couldn't get over it. Said it was the best thing they'd seen on their whole tour. Better than the Lincoln Memorial at night.

JIM

Oh yeah? I've seen that.

TED

Do you know that man cried?

JIM

What man?

TED

The man from Hawaii. Cried like a baby at the end.
Said he wasn't ashamed to admit it. Oh, the end is really
something—wait till you see it! During Pickett's Charge,
the tears poured down his face, seeing all those young
men cut down in their prime.

JIM

It's supposed to be women who cry over that. Maybe
statehood's gone to Hawaii's head.

> (*A backstage phone buzzes and the monitor
> light next to it blinks on and off*)

TED

I have to start the show.

JIM
(Impatient)

Now look, I gotta get back to the office.

TED

All I have to do is start it. It only takes a minute.

JIM

Well make it snappy. I'll wait for you outside.

TED

Oh I can't leave while a show is on! I never leave while
a show is on.

JIM

You said it was automatic—

—all kinds of things could happen. A fuse could blow. Anything. That's what I get paid for. Besides, there's that trouble with the volume.

> (HE *heads for the control booth*)

I'll just be a second.

JIM
> *(Mumbling to himself)*

Jesus Christ!

> (TED *is in the control booth.* HE *dims the stage lights, then flicks the tape recorder on. A smooth, husky* VOICE *comes out over the amplifying system)*

VOICE

Good evening, ladies and gentlemen. We welcome you to the Gettysburg National Monument and its famous Electric Map. You are located here,

> (*A white bulb on the Map flicks on and off*)

at the center of one of the world's great battlefields, now the site of the nation's eternal light peace memorial.

> (*The same white light flickers on and off again*)

We will now replay the Battle of Gettysburg for you on the Electric Map, so that later, when you go out on the battlefield, you will be able to locate your position—and also that of the Enemy.

> (*Phony chuckle*)

Depending, of course, on which side you think *is* the Enemy.

The battlefield measures six miles North and South

58

*(Large white bulbs on North/South border
of the map light up)*

and seven miles East and West.

*(Large white bulbs on East/West border
of the map light up)*

On July 1, 1863, General Robert E. Lee, leading the
Confederate Army in an invasion of the North, pauses in
his march north and west of the town of Gettysburg.

*(The red bulbs on the north and west side of
the Map flicker on and off to indicate Lee's
position)*

General George Meade, commander of the Union forces,
takes up a position south of the town of Gettysburg, to
defend any possible thrust at Washington, D.C., the
federal capitol.

*(The blue bulbs on the southern side of the
Map flicker on and off to indicate Meade's
position)*

The first engagement of the two opposing armies comes
when Heth's division moves forward to make a
reconnaissance

*(Red bulbs start to flicker to indicate Heth's
position)*

and finds itself met by Buford's cavalry division.

*(Blue bulbs start to flicker to indicate
Buford's position)*

Buford sends back word to Meade requesting Union
reinforcements.

*(Other blue bulbs start flickering and move
toward the bulbs indicating Buford's
division)*

59

The Confederates, too, move in reinforcements.
> (*Other red bulbs start flickering and move toward the bulbs indicating Heth's position*)

The Confederates now begin a two-fold attack on the Union position at Seminary Ridge. One column drives in from the northeast and starts eating up the Union flank. The Federals try to stay in position, but the two-pronged attack soon drives them to the opposite sides of the Valley . . .
> (TED *comes out of the control booth*)

TED
> (*Shouting over the* VOICE)

What do you think? Isn't it something?

JIM
> (*Shouting back*)

Turn the Goddamn volume down!
> (TED *goes over to the monitor and turns it down*)

TED

I had the monitor on so you could hear the show.

JIM

How the hell do you expect us to talk with all that noise?

TED

It's off now.
> (*Pause*)

JIM

Whose voice is it?

TED

The voice on the tape?

JIM

Yeah. Sounds a little like you.

TED

Oh no. It's a professional actor. At least he was.
Somebody said he's an airline pilot now.

JIM

I'll bet you know the whole speech by heart.

TED

Sure. If the sound went out, I could pick right up with
the microphone. It's never happened, though.

JIM

Mmm. Just as well, I suppose. Your voice is wrong. I
told you that when you were a kid.

(Pause)

Now, let's get down to business. Warren is *not* fine. I
want the facts.

TED

(Hesitantly)

It's not anything very . . . I mean, well . . . we're in
a little trouble.

JIM

So I gather.

TED

It's sort of . . . serious.

JIM

You're not dragging me into this! Is that clear? I got a lot
at stake in this town.

TED

You *are* my brother.

61

JIM

Let's not put *that* broken record on. We had the same
parents. Period.

(*Chuckles*)

And I wouldn't swear to that.

TED

I don't think that's funny.

JIM

I don't either.

TED

You could show some respect for mama's memory.

(JIM *laughs*)

JIM

What about papa's memory?

TED

Yes, his too. You could show some respect.

(JIM *gestures toward the Map*)

JIM

You take care of the memories.

TED

If mama was alive you wouldn't say these things.

(JIM *laughs in amazement*)

JIM

Thirty-six years old and still at it with the old lady!

TED

You wouldn't and you know it.

JIM

Wouldn't *what?*

TED

Wouldn't say something like that to mama's face.

JIM

You mean *you* wouldn't. I said plenty to her face, in case you forgot.

TED
(Resentful)

I remember. I remember very well.

JIM

Glad to hear it.

TED

That's why she told you to leave. You were always making trouble.

JIM
(Getting angry)

Is that right.

TED

So she told you to clear out.

JIM

Nobody *told* me to leave. I left. Period.

TED

You cried. Hard.

(JIM is flustered. HE tries to make light of it)

JIM

Are you kidding? I couldn't wait to get out of that place.

TED

Then why'd you keep asking to come back?

(JIM snorts)

63

JIM

Who told you that horseshit?

TED

Nobody told me that horseshit. I was there.

JIM

If I'd ever set one foot in that house again, it would have been too soon.

TED

Well, it's just as well, Jimmy, 'cause you weren't missed.
(The VOICE *on the amplifier suddenly becomes audible)*

VOICE

To sum up the first day: Union forces had been driven back through—

TED

(Over the VOICE*)*
Don't go, Jim! Please! I didn't mean it.
*(*HE *starts toward the control booth)*
Just let me fix the volume. Don't go! Please!

VOICE

—Gettysburg streets and alleys to seek temporary security from the slashing attack, and ended up *right here* where we are located.
(The white bulb flickers on and off. Then the stage lights slowly dim)
During the night, the Confederate lines begin to re-form. Reinforcements arrive from the west.
(New red bulbs on the Map light up)

64

General Longstreet's corps, delayed for two days, reaches camp during the night and takes up a position . . .

> *(The volume goes down to inaudible.* TED *comes out of the control booth)*

TED
(Subdued)
You see what I mean? The volume suddenly jumps.
(Pause)
I'm sorry for what I said. I didn't mean it, Jimmy.

JIM
(Still angry)
Didn't mean what?!

TED
That we didn't miss you.
(Trying to snow him) ˙
When you left, I cried. I remember that.

JIM
You were grinning from ear to ear.

TED
Me?!! Oh no, not me!

JIM
No? Maybe it was her. The two of you get mixed up.

TED
(With false feeling)
She felt bad, Jimmy. Real bad. She talked about you all the time.

JIM
I'll bet.

65

TED

She *did*.

> (*A small amount of activity begins on the Map. Two or three red bulbs flicker and move forward. Two or three blue bulbs then flicker and move forward to meet the advancing red bulbs*)

JIM

Look, I don't give a shit. It's thirty years ago. I didn't give a shit then.

> (*The bulbs on the Map flicker a few times and then go out*)

What the hell's the matter with the lights?

TED

It's night.

JIM

What?

TED

It's night on the battlefield.

JIM

It's like a tomb in here.

TED

> (*Trying to change the subject; false cheer*)

Hey, I got a great idea!

> (HE *moves toward his footlocker*)

How about a little snort, huh?

JIM

I thought you couldn't leave.

TED

Don't have to leave. I keep a little something right here.
A little pick-me-up, as mama used to say. Two plastic
cups and a little Old Grand Dad.

JIM
(*Friendlier*)
Old Grand Dad! Shit, even your bourbon's got whiskers
on it.

TED
(*Calling from the locker*)
What?

JIM
That's expensive bourbon.

(TED *comes back to center stage*)

TED
What the hell—you're my brother, aren't you?
(HE *pours the drinks*)
It's been months since we got together. This is like a
reunion.

(HE *hands* JIM *his drink, then raises his
glass*)
Here we go. To us—to brothers! As mama used to say,
blood's thicker than water.

JIM
Maybe that's why it clots so easy.

TED
(*False appreciation*)
Same old character!

67

JIM

Here's blood in your eye.

> (THEY *belt the drinks.* TED *shudders after drinking*)

TED

Whew! Nice, huh?

JIM

It's good stuff. The old lady got you into *some* good habits.

> (TED *laughs nervously*)

TED

She sure knew how to hold her liquor, didn't she!

JIM

She practiced a lot.

TED

> (*Trying to keep it light*)

Do you know she never touched a drop during the day? Did you know that?

JIM

I didn't follow her habits too close. The parties were beauts. I remember those.

TED

> (*Defensive*)

Mama never had parties. Just a friend in now and then.

JIM

Two people can make a lot of noise. It gets to sound like a party. Anyway, how would you know? You were always sent to Don and Bobbie's for the night.

> (TED *reacts as if hit.* HE *goes for the bourbon*)

68

TED

How about another?

JIM

Not for me.

> (TED *pours himself another drink.* JIM, *needling*)

Good old Don and Bobbie. I wonder whatever happened to Don and Bobbie.

> (TED *belts his second drink, then shudders again*)

TED

Oh-h-h! Nice.

JIM

Whaddaya think ever happened to Don and Bobbie, huh?

TED

They were nice men.

JIM

Oh yeah? In what way?

TED

> *(Evasive)*

Nice. Pleasant. You know.

> *(Abrupt shift)*

Hey!—I'm going to treat myself! I've been a good boy. And this has been sort of a tough day. Yes sir, this has been *sort* of a tough day.

JIM

"Sweet." Isn't that what mama used to call them? "Real sweet men."

69

TED

I don't like the way you talk about mama.

JIM

I'm talking about Don and Bobbie.

(TED *swallows his third drink*)

JIM

They were real convenient for mama. When "company" came, off went her little Teddy to Don and Bobbie's for the night. She used to say the three of you looked "cute" together. You do remember going to Don and Bobbie's, don't you?

TED

Sort of.

JIM

This town's got a lotta bad memories for you. You should get away from Gettysburg.

(*Pause; menacing*)

Soon.

TED

I like Gettysburg. I do important work here.

JIM
(*Sadistically*)

If we could find out where Don and Bobbie were, maybe we could send you there. I mean, since they were such nice men, you'd get a kick out of seeing them again, right?

TED
(*Sullen*)

I don't even remember Don and Bobbie.

70

JIM

Now isn't that funny. And you over their place at least once a week.

TED

I was a kid. It's all kind of blurred.

JIM

You weren't a kid. You were twelve. That's why the old man stepped in.

TED
(Abrupt venom)
You're the one who stepped in.

JIM

So you do remember.

TED
(Shaking his head "no")
Nah.
(HE laughs, a little drunkenly)
I only remember what you make up. Ha! Ha!

JIM

I don't make anything up.

TED

That's what I said—I don't remember anything.
Ha! Ha!

JIM

It *was* me who stepped in.
(Pause)
And I'm going to step in again. But this time I'm not telling it to mama. I'm telling it to you.

71

TED

Let's not get back to mama.

JIM

That's right. We're gonna stick to you and Warren.

TED

Mama was a lovely lady. You never appreciated mama.

JIM

Forget mama!

TED

You shouldn't make up stories. Let the dead lie.

JIM

Here's to that! Let's not build tombs for 'em either: too
many people get locked inside.

> (*The lights suddenly come up.* JIM *looks
> around, startled*)

Now what?

TED

It's the second day.

JIM

Huh?

TED

It's dawn of the second day.

> (*Lapsing into monotone*)

If the Confederates attack early, they stand a good
chance of success. But Longstreet is against an offensive.
He argues stubbornly with Lee.

JIM

> (*Low*)

Okay. Okay.

TED

Lee is patient. He hears Longstreet out. It is eleven
A.M. before Lee finally orders Longstreet to attack.

JIM
(Louder)

Cut it out, willya? I don't have to hear this shit.

TED

By then it is too late. Meade has fortified his position.
The federal—

JIM
(Interrupting)

Hey—enough! Christ, once you get started, you're hard
to stop!

TED

If you stop, you lose track. It's like typing: if you *think*
about the keys, you've had it. You got to keep going.
(Pause; then a trace of contempt)

You don't know who Longstreet is, do you.

JIM
(Belligerently)

That's right, I don't.
(Pause)

Now look. I want the facts about what happened last
night. What was Warren doing in the bus depot?

TED
(Evasive)

Warren's a good boy. He's a good boy at heart.

JIM

What was he doing?

73

TED

He's only a boy.

JIM

I'm the one who told you that when you took him in, remember?

TED

The boy needed a home.
(Barbed)
Every boy needs a home.

JIM

Every boy needs a mother *and* a father.

TED
(Petulantly)
I do what I can for Warren. I don't bother you. I got problems, but I handle them.
*(*JIM *laughs sardonically)*
And don't think this job isn't a handful. This is a monument. A national monument. Millions of people come here to—

> *(*HE *stops in mid-sentence in reaction to trumpet blasts over the amplifier and the lights suddenly going up and down—as they might during a cannonading)*

It's Little Round Top! Oh wait'll you see this!

> *(*HE *starts toward the monitor)*

I'll turn the monitor up so you don't miss it.

JIM

Now look, I told you I want—

74

TED

—I always listen to this part! It only takes a second!

> (HE *turns up the sound volume on the
> monitor*)

VOICE

Meade's chief engineer, Brigadier General Gouveneur
K. Warren is the first to see the strategic importance of
Little Round Top. From its height Confederate guns
could command all the ground between it and our
position here.

> (*The white bulb flickers on and off again.*
> JIM *looks at* TED *with exasperation, then
> starts to pace the stage*)

Warren rushes reinforcements to Little Round Top.
Not a moment too soon. Fifteen minutes later, the
Confederates charge.

> (*Red bulbs move toward Little Round
> Top*)

They are repulsed with great bloodshed, but they re-
form and charge again.

> (*Red bulbs move back to signal Confederate
> retreat, then, simultaneously with trumpet
> blasts, move forward again to signal second
> advance*)

The carnage is terrible; it is a high point of the heroic
struggle. The Union forces, led by General Dan Sickles,
suffer four thousand casualties in two hours. The First
Minnesota loses eighty-two percent of its men within
fifteen minutes.

> (*Some of the bulbs go out*)

75

General Sickles himself is struck by a **Confederate** shell which leaves his right leg hanging in shreds, the thighbone exposed.

> *(One blue bulb flickers on and off; then stays on)*

But Sickles lives! Indeed he will outlive all other corps commanders, not dying till fifty-one years later, in 1914.

> *(The lights start to dim. Muffled drum rolls)*

And so night falls on the bloody scene.

> *(*TED *starts to lower the volume on the monitor)*

The field is strewn with corpses, but none has died in vain. They have given their all to defend their principles, each man dying nobly for his . . .

> *(The volume is now inaudible)*

TED

That part always moves me. No matter how many times I hear it.

JIM

What was Warren doing?

TED
(Still mesmerized)

Doing?! Saving the battle, that's all! The whole *war*! If he hadn't realized that Little Round Top—

JIM
(Interrupting)

—*your* Warren.

76

TED

(Confused)

My Warren?

(HE giggles)

Oh! *My* Warren. Nothing. He wasn't doing anything.

JIM

(Exasperated)

That's not what the morning paper says.

TED

(Horrified)

You mean it's in the—

JIM

—that's exactly what I mean.

TED

What does it say?

JIM

It says that the police are looking for a Warren G. Rucker of Ninety-seven Fall Street for resisting arrest last night at the bus depot.

(HE throws the paper at TED)

Have the police been to see you?

TED

Chief Bradford came to the house last night. I told him Warren had left town, that I didn't know where he was.

(Brightening)

But I do know, Jim. He's gone to New York. I know where he is. You can help me get him back. You know everybody in town. You've got influence. You could talk to Chief Bradford.

JIM

Do you know you're goddamn lucky *your* name isn't in the paper. We're all lucky. And I intend to keep it that way.

TED

Warren made a mistake, that's all. He's a good boy. You know he is. It's just that he needed money. All kids need money. They have a lot to do. They—

JIM
(Interrupting)
Let's have it straight. Warren stole some money and was trying to skip town, when the police caught up with him at the bus depot.

TED
(Indignant)
That's a terrible thing to say! Warren's no thief! You could show a little more respect, you know. You shouldn't talk about Warren that way.

JIM
Then you talk about him.
(Pause)

TED
(Nervous)
Well, he . . . he . . . needed money.

JIM
You said that.

TED
There aren't many ways a seventeen-year-old can make money.

78

JIM

He's not seventeen. He was seventeen when he moved in
with you three years ago.

TED

Yes, well that's what I meant. Around that age it's hard
to make money.

JIM

Lots of twenty-year-olds manage. Why didn't you get
him a job here?

TED

He gets bored easy.
(Brightly)
But he likes the Map. He came here one day when he
first moved in. Sat through two showings in a row. Said
it was "a groove." But he never came back. He did work
for a week at the supermarket. But they made him a
checker, and he didn't like punching the register all day.
It made him feel like a machine, he said. I couldn't
blame him: he was getting fat, sitting all—

JIM
(Interrupting)
Get to the point.

TED

Yes. Well he, he met a tourist last summer. Down at the
bus depot. You know how the tourists are—lots of
money.

JIM

He's not supposed to show tourists around the battlefield.
That's a union job.

79

TED

Oh no, he didn't do that. He wouldn't do that.

JIM

Well, what *did* he do?

TED

The tourist, you see, was an older man. He, uh, took a shine to Warren. Rented a car. They took a drive together. But not the battlefield! They didn't drive around the battlefield! When it was over, he told Warren he was grateful for his . . . company . . . and gave him—

JIM
(Interrupting; exasperated)

When *what* was over?! Grateful for *what*, for Christ's sake?! Look, for once in your life, can you talk straight?

TED

You know what happened! Why should I have to say what happened! You're trying to upset me, that's all.

JIM
(Menacingly)

Say it.

(Pause)

TED

Warren was keeping an old gentleman company. Warren's a lively boy. Older people like that. No harm in it.

JIM

So. Little Warren was peddling his ass.

(TED doesn't answer)

Once or often?

80

TED

He got to hanging around the bus depot. Especially in
the warm weather.

JIM

In other words: often. Did you know about it?

TED

I came home one day in the middle of the afternoon. I
wasn't feeling well. They had to cancel a show.
(Enthusiastically shifting topics)
That never happened to me before. In seven years, I
hadn't missed a single show. Imagine: seven years, eight
times a day. And not one absence.

JIM

In other words you walked in on Warren and one of
his old men.

TED

(Resentful)
They were just resting. It was part of their drive.

JIM

Sounds like Warren had a nice little concession
going—just like all the local merchants in Gettysburg.
Except he was selling unauthorized souvenirs.

TED

Go away. Just go away. You don't want to help.

JIM

I'm going to help all right.
(HE takes money out of his wallet)
I'm going to help all of us.
(Waving the money)

81

You see this? Take it—take all of it. You buy you a one-way ticket out of this town.

TED

If you think I'm going to leave the Map, you've got to be crazy.

JIM

You're the one who's crazy. The police are involved!

TED

That was not Warren's fault!

JIM
(Wearily)
How did the police get into it?

TED

Warren started talking to a man in the depot. Suggested they take a drive. The man turned out to be a detective, from Harrisburg. He tried to grab Warren. Said he was going to turn him in to Chief Bradford. Warren had to get loose. He hit the detective. Hard. He was bleeding. Warren's a strong boy.

JIM
(Softly)
Jesus!

TED

I got to get him back, Jim. You could talk to Bradford. He likes you. Tell him the detective tried to pick Warren up. Tell him anything. He'll believe you. He likes you.

(The volume on the amplifier suddenly comes up)

82

VOICE

Having lost a golden opportunity to destroy the Union
line,

    (TED heads toward the control booth)

the Confederates end their attack for the night.

TED

He likes you. He really likes you.

    (HE goes into the control booth)

VOICE

This brings us to the morning of the third and final day
of the battle,

    (The lights start to go up)

to the turning point

    (Pause)

in the Civil War. Lee decides on a frontal assault. He
chooses George Pickett to lead it. Pickett is known
chiefly for the elegance of his clothes. His dark-brown
hair hangs from his shoulders in ringlets, which he keeps
carefully perfumed. Fifteen years earlier, in the . . .

    *(The volume is now inaudible; TED comes
    out of the control booth)*

TED

I don't know what's going on. The volume's gone crazy.
Up and down. I can't keep it under control. What am I
going to do?

JIM

It's all right now. Forget it. There's something I want to
tell you.

TED

You've got to help me. You've got to fix it. You know
about these things.

JIM

No, I don't. I can't help you. That's what I want to say. I
can't help you.

TED
(*Getting more upset*)
You *have* to help me! You *owe* it to me!

JIM

I owe you *nothing.* You've got one choice and only one.
You get out of Gettysburg—for good.
(*The volume suddenly jumps again; this
time it is even louder*)

VOICE

At three in the afternoon, Pickett's long gray lines start
moving toward the Union troops on the ridge a mile
away.

TED

Oh, Christ! What am I going to do?!
(HE *hurries into the control booth*)

VOICE

The Confederates walk straight into a murderous
barrage of Union fire.
(*Red and blue lights flicker and then
converge on the Map.* TED *yells out from the
control booth*)

TED

Jim, help me!

84

JIM

It's your goddamn monument, not mine!

VOICE

Some Confederates break ranks and run. One Tennessee sergeant will later admit, "For about a hundred yards I broke the lightning speed records. But then my conscience got the better of me. I was afraid of being shot in the back and disgracing my family forever."

(JIM *goes into the booth and starts fiddling with the controls*)

Two men from a North Carolina regiment actually reach the ridge. The Union soldiers hold their fire. "Come over to this side of the Lord!" a Union soldier shouts. The two Southerners cross over and surrender, grateful for the mercy shown.

(*A corny hymn, like* "Nearer My God to Thee," *starts playing softly*)

But for most there is no mercy, only death. Attempts are made to rally the troops for a renewed assault, but . . .

(*The volume suddenly goes off*)

JIM

Best I can tell, there's a short in one of the auditorium speakers. It's okay now, but it'll probably go again. You ought to kill it and pick up with the mike.

(HE *hands the mike to* TED)

TED
(*Terrified*)

No, it's okay now!

JIM

It's bound to go again.

85

TED

I don't care. It's near the end. I'll take a chance.

JIM

Have it your way. I got to get back.

TED

Will you speak to Bradford?

JIM

No.

TED

No?! How can you say no?!

JIM

I said it. There's nothing I can do.

TED

You could talk to Bradford. Tell him it's all a mistake.
Mistaken identity—yes, that's it, mistaken identity.

JIM
(Softly)

That's what it is all right.

TED

How'll I get Warren back?

JIM

You won't get Warren back.
(Pause)
You'll be lucky if they don't take you in, too.

TED
(Smothered rage)

You'd like that, wouldn't you?

JIM

I gave you my advice: pack it in.

(Gesturing to encompass the Map)

Close the door on the whole goddamn thing!

TED

(Getting hysterical)

That's enough, you hear me?! That's enough!

(JIM puts his hands on TED's shoulders, as if to quiet him)

JIM

If you want to survive, forget Warren and *get out of Gettysburg*. Otherwise you're going to end up in jail yourself.

(TED breaks away)

TED

You'd like to see me in jail, back in the State Home, wouldn't you? Well I'm not going back, you hear? I'm not going back to jail just to make you happy!

JIM

What the hell are you talking about now?

TED

Don't think I don't know why mama sent me to the Home. I know you were behind it. I've always known you were behind it.

(A sudden bleep from the amplifier; the volume comes up loud)

VOICE

No one will ever be able to tally the suffering, the high hopes destroyed, the young men cut down in their prime.

87

JIM

Will you get in there and stop that noise!

(The amplifier bleeps again; the volume goes down)

TED

I know why I got sent to the Home, taken away from mama!

JIM

If you don't get hold of yourself, they're going to carry you out of here.

TED

You told her what was going on with Don and Bobbie! You told her to send me to the Home, or you'd go to the police. You made mama send me away! You're the one who separated me and mama!

.

JIM
(Quietly)
No one could ever do that.

TED

You did it! I know you did it! And all because she loved *me*!

(JIM grabs TED and throws him against the railing of the Map. TED crumbles)

JIM

Now listen, you! I've about had it with your bullshit. With your fucking Warrens, and your maps, and your mamas! Do you want to know what *really* happened?! You want to hear the *true* story for a change?!

88

TED

Just get out of here, that's all. Leave me alone. Just leave me alone.

JIM

You are alone. You and your make-believe world.

TED

Get out of here!!

JIM

I did tell mama I'd go to the police if she didn't stop shipping you over to Don and Bobbie. And you know what? She said I should go right ahead. She wouldn't mind at all if they took you off to the State Boys' Home. You get it? She was glad for the chance to get rid of you. You were a nuisance. You got in the way when she wanted to fuck with the garage mechanic or the delivery man. *She wanted to get rid of you!*

(TED *turns to face* JIM)

TED

You bastard. You lying bastard.

(TED *suddenly lunges at* JIM)

I'll kill you! I'll kill you!

(THEY *grapple.* JIM *throws* TED *to the floor.* TED *gets up, and weeping goes to* JIM *and tries to embrace him.* JIM *knees* TED *in the groin.* TED *doubles over in pain on the floor)*

JIM

Don't touch me—you freak.

(HE *heads for the exit)*

89

TED
She loved me. She loved me.

JIM
She's yours. You can have her.

(HE *gestures to the Map*)

You can have all of them. All your pretty pictures. None of them are real, anyway. You don't even exist.

(JIM *exits*)

TED
(*Shouting after* JIM)
She hated *you!* She hated *you!*

(*The Map goes wild. Loud noises from the amplifier, mixed with words*)

VOICE
On the Union side there is wild rejoicing . . . zzz . . . mmm . . . grinning soldiers everywhere . . . trailing Rebel flags in the dirt . . . zzz . . . mmm . . . "That'll hold the bastards!" "That'll hold 'em . . . " zzz . . . mmm . . .

(*Bulbs flicker all over the Map.* TED *starts to get up off the floor; realizes* HE *must get to the control booth*)

. . . cheers and yells . . . zzzz . . . mmmm . . . zzz . . . victory dance . . . zzz . . . mmm . . . zzz . . . General Hays grabs and kisses a young lieutenant on his staff . . . zzzz . . . mmmm . . . zzzzz . . . "Give me a flag, boy! . . . Give me a flag!" . . . zzz . . . mmm . . . zzz . . . mmm . . . zzz.

(TED *is now in the control booth*)

90

"We've broke 'em all to hell . . . broke 'em all to hell!"
zzz . . . mmm . . .

> (TED *shuts off the controls. The volume goes
> dead. The lights on the Map, and most of
> the stage lights, go out, leaving* TED *in
> semi-darkness. For a few seconds, there
> is absolute quiet.* TED *looks upstage through
> the Map into the "auditorium."* HE *grabs
> the script of the "show" from above the
> control booth and tries to find his place
> in it. Then, trembling,* HE *picks up the
> microphone)*

> TED
> (HIS *voice barely under control)*

Ladies and gentlemen . . . this is very unfortunate
. . . never in seven years . . . this is the first time in
seven years that we have not . . . that our equipment
has not functioned. The battle, in any case, is almost
over . . . if you will bear with me . . . if you will try
to help me . . . I will attempt to finish up . . . to tell
you . . . what happened . . .
"It was an accident of birth and environment" . . . I
mean . . .

> (HE *searches frantically for his place in the
> script; then, reading from it)*

I mean, as the motto on the memorial says . . . nobody
could help it . . . "The Accident of Birth and
Environment Determined Whether They Would Wear
the Blue or Gray." All were good boys. All of them . . .
good at heart . . .
And now that it's over, *all finished* . . . Robert E. Lee

91

blames only himself . . . nobody else. As the survivors
stagger back across the bloody field, Lee rides out among
them and speaks to them. They are crazed with fear until
they hear his voice. "His fault," he says over and over
again, "his fault." He comforts them like a good parent, a
good mama . . . He gathers them to him. They hug his
leg. Their blood streaks over his white horse. He does
not send them away. She would not send him away . . .
She was a good woman, a lovely woman . . . she
would not send him away . . .

(HE *returns to the script*)

The battlefield is dark. Lee rides back to his
headquarters. It is all over, all over . . . "Too bad; too
bad, Oh, too bad!" . . . "We must find the way home,"
Lee says, "home to Virginia." . . . "Home," he keeps
saying, "we must find our way home now . . ."

(TED *struggles to control himself*)

That, ladies and gentlemen, is the end of our story, the
end of the last day of the battle.

(HE *switches on the stage lights. All the
bulbs on the Map suddenly light up*)

We hope you have enjoyed your visit to the Electric
Map, and that you will have a pleasant day touring the
battlefield . . .

We close this performance, as is our custom, with lines
from the speech Abraham Lincoln made on this same
spot . . . four and one-half months after Robert E. Lee
led his men home to Virginia . . . lines that even today
echo through the free world, giving hope and courage to
all mankind.

92

(TED *flicks another switch and* "The Battle Hymn of the Republic" *starts playing in the background. At the same time the colors of some of the bulbs on the Map change so that they are of equal proportions of red, white and blue. They all start to flicker simultaneously. The official* VOICE *comes out over the amplifier*)

VOICE

. . . testing whether that nation, or any nation so conceived . . . zzz . . .

(*Static interrupts the speech.* TED *reacts with horror at the realization that even the Lincoln tape is defective. Through the remainder of the speech, as the static and volume grow in intensity, so too does* TED*'s desperate jiggling of the control knobs and his pounding on the sides of the booth*)

We have come to dedicate a . . . zzz . . . mmm . . . final resting place for those who . . . zzz . . . mmm . . . It is for us, the living rather, to be dedicated . . . zzz . . . mmm . . . to the great task remaining before us—that from these honored dead we take increased devotion . . . zzzzzz . . . mmmmmm . . . zzzzzz . . . here highly resolve . . . zzz . . . mmmm . . . zzzzzz

(*As the bleeps, noise and static drown out the address, the* "Battle Hymn" *and the red, white and blue lights reach their climax.* TED, *near collapse, grabs the microphone*)

93

. : . and that government of the people, by the people, for the people, shall not perish from the earth.

TED
(Shouting hysterically into the mike)
She was a lovely lady!! She hated him!!
(As the static and the music peak)

THE CURTAIN FALLS